Please return/renew this item by the last date
shown. Books may also be renewed by
telephoning, writing to or calling in at any of
our libraries or on the internet.

Northamptonshire Libraries and Information Service

Northamptonshire
County Council

www.library.northamptonshire.gov.uk/catalogue

Visit
www.how2become.com
for more business titles
and career guides

Orders: Please contact how2become Ltd, Suite 2, 50 Churchill Square Business Centre, Kings Hill, Kent ME19 4YU. You can also order via the e-mail address info@how2become.co.uk

ISBN: 9781909229631

First published 2013

Copyright © 2013 Glen Topping. All rights reserved.

Contents

CHAPTER 1

Introduction

GETTING STARTED

You will need to allocate adequate time and resources to get your business up and running. You will need to set time and money aside to ensure your business is set up properly and professionally. Early and thorough organisation of both your business and your time will pay dividends later on and help to ensure success.

In addition, when you are starting your new business, it is very important to remain committed, energetic and enthusiastic about your new venture. Do not undertake all the work yourself unless you have to. Do seek help and advice from friends and family in order that you can get your business organised and set up most effectively.

This guide should be read in conjunction with many other sources of information to help you succeed in setting up and running a successful and profitable business.

10 REASONS WHY BUSINESSES FAIL

1. Starting your business for the wrong reasons – If the only reason you want to start your own business is to make a

million pounds, or to spend more time at home, or because you just want to be your own boss, then you may need to ask yourself more questions.

However, if you want to start your own business for the following reasons, then you will have a better chance of business success:

a) You know you will enjoy what you will be doing and you believe that it will work. If you enjoy what you do, you will be naturally good at it.

b) You are a strong individual who enjoys a challenge and won't take 'No' for an answer.

c) You have researched your product and your market and understand the area of business.

d) You learn from your mistakes and use these lessons to succeed the next time around. Believe it or not, many successful and famous business people have experienced failure first time round.

e) You are patient, financially astute and have a positive outlook.

f) You have an eye for detail and can put yourself in your customers' shoes and you like to do things right.

g) You are a good communicator and have a good level of emotional intelligence. You essentially get on with most people.

2. Lack of financial backing/security – A frequent mistake made by many businesses is the lack of money to start up the business or lack of operational funding to run the business.

It is easy to underestimate how much money is required to operate and run your business venture. You need to do your homework!

It is essential to get the correct level of financial backing or initial investment, not only the costs of starting, but the costs of running the business. It is important to consider the operating costs and day to day running. This means you will need enough funding to cover your operating costs until your commissions or sales can eventually pay for these costs.

3. Poor research – If you have ever managed any sort of project or event, you will know that it requires a lot of careful thinking and planning. In addition to this, there will always be things that go wrong and you must be prepared for these events.

Your idea needs to be turned into a plan of action or a business plan. What's your market? Who are your customers? How are you going to market the business? These are the sort of questions that you must ask yourself over and over again until you come up with answers, which can then be incorporated into your business plan.

4. Lack of business management – New business owners often lack the correct expertise to run a business. All businesses require expertise or skills in financial planning and management, purchasing and supply, marketing, managing staff and good communication skills.

Lack of attention to your business can also lead to the demise of your business. You must regularly review, organise, plan and control all activities and keep an active eye on your competitors.

A successful business owner is also a good manager and a natural leader who creates a work ethic that encourages productivity. A good leader is also a strategic thinker who is able to turn a vision into a reality, able to confront change and look toward the future.

5. Not keeping your business up to date and unique – Your business is more likely to succeed if you have a unique selling point (USP). Many businesses do not and therefore do not stand out from the crowd. Ensuring that you have a USP and that your business is up to date will most certainly help prevent failure.

6. Poor business location – Location, both physical and virtual, is critical to the success of any business. If you are going to have a shop front, then you will need a good footfall of potential customers to get noticed. A bad location can be fatal if your business relies simply upon passing trade.

Considerations should include:

- Where your customers are and where you operate
- Passing traffic, parking and lighting
- Competitors' operational areas
- First impressions of your premises (neat & tidy)
- Local grants and funding schemes for employers
- Past use of the building
- Security and accessibility
- Local community

7. Incorrect pace of business growth – Businesses need to grow but this must be at a manageable pace. Expand too fast and the business will not be able to cope and customers will complain or you will burn out. You must focus on slow steady growth, managed at the right pace. Many a bankruptcy has been caused by businesses growing to fast.

Review your growth plans regularly and identify what and who you need to add in order for your business to grow. Then, with the right systems and people in place, you can focus on the growth of your business and not on doing everything yourself.

8. No Internet presence – The worldwide web is expanding rapidly and your business needs to have a presence on it. Whatever you sell, do or trade, you should have a website. Websites can grow your business revenue and, in addition, can also be useful revenue streams. It is important that you also use the web for advertising as more and more people are choosing it to source goods and services.

9. You – It does not take long for a business to fail and many businesses fail because the owner or proprietor does not engage fully with the business. You are the 'secret' to your success. For many successful business owners, failing is never an option. With right drive, determination and hard work, you can and will succeed in business.

10. Not listening to the professionals – Business is complex. There are taxes, laws, procedures, government and ever changing circumstances to which we have to adapt. Don't be afraid to change, but you must take advice from experts and follow all the good advice you can. If it's free, then grab it with both hands – knowledge is power. Listen to your

suppliers, customers and accountants to ensure that your business does not fail.

THE CLEANING BUSINESS

The great thing about owning your own business and being your own boss is the ability of being able to work when you want and how you want. This can make a difference to your life work balance and of course your financial situation. Owning and running your own business will allow you to do as much or as little as you like when you like and how you like. Much of your day will be determined by you through good planning and control of your days and weeks ahead.

Don't underestimate it! Being your own boss can often be stressful and difficult. But with it, is your opportunity to earn money with no limits. You'll be challenged daily but this guide will give you the tools and skills required to set up your own Cleaning Business.

Many people often dream of starting their own cleaning business but that's where the dream often ends. But those people that have become successful in business and in life are the people who have put their dreams and plans into action by doing what they dream about. By committing yourself to starting your business and putting in the hours and effort required there is no reason why you cannot operate and run a successful business in this industry.

You must be prepared to keep your customers interests at heart as a business such as this will require you to be flexible friendly and adaptable to meet your customers needs. Much of this business is repeated through word of mouth which

can often be the best way to own and operate a successful business. This type of business is built by reputation and can often lead to repeat work without advertising. A good cleaning company is always in demand. Customers want fast and effective service at a reasonable cost. Remember this and you won't go far wrong.

Whether your client is a commercial organisation or a domestic customer, you should always strive to provide an excellent service to all of your clients!

THE CLEANING INDUSTRY

The cleaning industry has been around for many years, since very early days, the rich and local gentry employed the services of cleaners and maids to clean their homes, shops and factories. Today the industry is worth billions in UK revenue each year and is still growing. This industry is a large economic indicator and employs hundreds and thousands each and every year. There are two distinct markets within the industry. The commercial market such as, shops, housing associations, local authorities, schools, college's hotels and holiday resorts, golf clubs and offices with large property portfolios. Through to the domestic market where residential householders requiring one off services of a cleaning contractor to blitz their new home to regular weekly cleans for the busy family or executive.

There are millions of commercial offices and workplaces in the UK, all of which require reliable cleaning services as well as massive demand in the domestic sector still.

This day and age, the commercial market often runs on a contractual basis offering the possibility of short or long-term contracts for property cleaning services which will improve your business cash flow and business prosperity. This sector is competitive though.

You may initially wish to sub contract for bigger clients whom have these corporate contracts, which may help you with cash flow and turnover, getting your business off the ground. The domestic market is often more casual, often without formal contracts being exchanged for the services offered.

To run a business such as this, you will need good communication skills and be physically fit. You will need to be organised and competent in the use of a computer, as these days much of any business involves technology.

Much of the equipment and stock required to run a business of this nature is widely available throughout the country to both hire and purchase. To get started you will need a reasonable amount of capital outlay and of course, some effort to promote and set up your business in the local area. Clearly you also need a form of transport to enable your equipment to be transported and excess waste to be removed. However, none of this needs to be expensive. There are many solutions that will enable you to carry out a business of this nature from your own home with very little room or capital outlay required.

Whether you are professionally qualified or have picked up your skills from years of practice, starting a business in this sector could not be easier as it is one which requires a good knowledge of the industry and key contacts to be really successful.

CHAPTER 2

Getting up and Running

FINANCING YOUR BUSINESS

Before you get going, you will need funding in order to buy stock, equipment and/or services required to get your business off the ground and start trading. There are many ways to obtain business finance and the most common are outlined below.

Bank Loans for Business

Obtaining a bank loan is still the most common form of borrowing, with a long and established history. Starting your

business with a loan can be a gamble and you must ensure that you will be able to pay back the amount agreed in the terms and conditions of the loan.

Business loans are often used to buy plant and materials and/or equipment in order that the business can operate.

The capital is, therefore, tied up in a tangible asset should the bank require the loan to be repaid. You are advised to ensure

that you seek professional advice before embarking upon taking out a loan. It is also wise to test the market to ensure that the loan that your lender is offering is competitive with other lenders.

Secured Loans are loans that are secured against an asset such as a premise or, in some cases, a private home. You are advised to think very carefully before embarking upon a loan of this nature and should discuss the issue of a standard or secured loan with a professional. You can obtain a list of professional financial advisers from the Financial Services Authority website www.fsa.gov.uk.

Using Savings to Help Start your Business

Many people use their savings in order to set up and run their business. This could be from saving over a long period, an inheritance or, maybe, a redundancy payment.

This is a great way of starting your business venture, as there is no cost to using your savings, other than the interest that would have been gained from having the money invested or saved elsewhere. If your business is financed in this way, with no or very little borrowing against it, it may make it more attractive to potential investors. This is a decision that only you can make and advice should be sought from professionals before investing a substantial amount of your own money into your business.

Attracting Investors in your Business

If you want financial investment in your business, you will need to put together a list of people, maybe friends, family or colleagues, who you think may be willing to invest time and money in your business. You need to think carefully about this before entering into negotiation, as this is a business venture and should not be dealt with in the same manner as a friendship.

People don't just give money away so you will need to clearly demonstrate what's in it for them. As well as your passion for your business, show your potential investor(s) your business plan and your ideas for making the business work. Let them know what is in it for them and what the likely timescales and profits are for the return on their investment. What are you offering them – stock, a profit share or a fixed return in a set period of time with some profit attached?

Your investor(s) will want to see the business growing and also be kept informed of how their investment is doing. Keep them on side and keep them updated as to where your business is going.

INSIDE TIP

In order to protect yourself and your investor(s), ensure you seek professional advice when entering into any agreement. Make sure that everyone is clear about expectations and that the agreement made is clear and simple. We recommend you speak to a solicitor to ensure the correct representation and advice is given.

Interest Free Credit

 You may find that some suppliers will offer you interest free credit in order to help get your business off the ground and established. In particular, suppliers offering start-up packages for your area of business will often give you the option of obtaining interest free credit. Clearly, this is an ideal way of borrowing as you will pay no interest on the loan you have undertaken to repay. This is of particular interest, for instance, if you were intending to purchase equipment with your savings, which can now be redirected and used to run the business. However, we advise that you ensure the agreements are in favour of your business.

Should you default on a loan of this nature, you may find that the interest and the payments can be affected dramatically. Always seek professional financial advice before embarking upon any borrowing and also ensure that the detail of the borrowing is clear, concise and in plain English.

Supplier Accounts

Setting up supplier accounts will be important to your business, allowing you to purchase goods or materials needed to operate the business. Your suppliers may offer various different accounts and you should, therefore, thoroughly check any terms and conditions in great detail before you commit.

This can be a good way of organising your business, especially if you have a high turnover of goods and services. For example, you can obtain your goods or materials on a 30,

60 or 90 day credit payment term with your supplier and start to sell before you are required to pay the supplier. If your turnover is consistent and quick, you will obviously obtain your profit element before being required to settle your account. You will need to ensure that your supplier limits are not breached and that you stay within the operating terms of the account agreed with the supplier.

Businesses can often experience problems with the reliability of suppliers, which can ultimately affect the efficiency of your business. Finding good suppliers with good account terms that suit your business will be essential in order to enable you to respond to your customers in an effective and reliable manner.

As you build up a payment history with your suppliers, you will often find that the account terms will grow with your business and the credit availability and terms of payment attached to your supplier account may increase. This will allow you to grow your business by increasing your stock availability, giving you a higher turnover.

We emphasise that you should always discuss any finance or credit facilities with an appropriately qualified individual to ensure that you are advised in a professional manner.

Working Capital for your Business

 You will obviously need funds 'working capital' in order to operate your business smoothly. When setting up your business, you will need to ensure you have enough working capital to run the business efficiently on a

day-to-day basis. It is not wise to run the business continually on a day-to-day basis on borrowed money.

WHAT WILL I NEED TO GET STARTED?

This section of the guide will outline what you need to get started in business and will cover the equipment itself, the administrative equipment required (e.g. booking diary, website, stationery, advertising material, transport) and professional guidance from people such as accountants, and, of course, the tax man.

Getting a personal computer (PC)

A computer will be a distinct advantage in setting up and running your business. Most people already own a computer, or some form of technology, which also allows them to access the Internet. If  you don't already own a computer, we recommend that you get one as soon as you can. This will help you to manage and run your business more effectively and, additionally, once connected to the Internet it could save you hundreds, maybe even thousands, of pounds. If you are not technically minded, then don't hesitate to seek advice on the right kind of computer that will suit your business. You may also need training.

There are many great deals available and a portable laptop computer can be just as powerful as a desktop computer. The advantages of a laptop are great. They are small, compact and fully portable, and, equipped with wireless Internet access enabling you to work anywhere you wish, on holiday, away from home, or simply somewhere peaceful.

A portable computer also allows you fast and ready access to the Internet, which is paramount if you are planning to have a website and e-mail, which the majority of businesses require. Most laptops are able to pick up wireless Internet networks which will enable you to access the Internet, your website and e-mail almost anywhere.

INSIDE TIP

*You may be able to obtain your laptop or **COMPUTER FOR FREE!** If you sign up to a monthly mobile broadband company for a fixed period of time. However, we recommend that you seek professional advice before entering into any agreement with broadband providers.*

Mobile broadband is a great way to access the Internet via your laptop anywhere you can receive a good signal, much like a mobile phone, and will enable you to access the Internet and your e-mail almost anywhere in the UK, dependent upon the provider.

INSIDE TIP

There are many different account packages and mobile broadband providers and you could try this very cheaply by simply purchasing a pay as you go service similar to a mobile phone provider. Then, once you are satisfied that mobile broadband is right for your business or complements your existing Internet landline provider, you can purchase a better value or more permanent plan.

Home/Office broadband connection

It is generally expected that any reputable business works with the Internet and we recommend that your business has a broadband connection as this will be the fastest and most reliable way of accessing the Internet from your home or office. You will need an existing landline which is live, which  most broadband providers will check to ensure that the services is provided in your area and that they can achieve the desired connection speed before you committing to any provider/contract.

INSIDE TIP

Finding a suitable broadband provider can be confusing and difficult and we recommend that you speak to a professional for advice. This can be done by simply visiting a few High Street shops (such as PC World) where you can obtain technical advice to help you make up your mind. Some popular Internet sites, such as www.money-savingexpert.com and www.moneysupermarket.com, have broadband provider comparison sites where you can compare Internet contract terms, broadband speeds, download limits and reliability data, etc., to help you make up your mind when choosing your provider.

Getting a good printer

You will need a good quality printer to enable you to produce letters, receipts, invoices, etc., and also to produce promotional material such as flyers or notices.

Laser printers are quite common and inexpensive to buy and run and we suggest you should buy a colour laser printer. These can be bought for around £130-£150 for printer of a high standard of print quality. They  can undertake big print runs of a high quality and can operate for long periods before renewal or placement of the toner.

INSIDE TIP
Ensure that the purchase and running costs are low as toner can often be expensive and, in some cases, as much as a printer. Check with your supplier on the cost of the toner and check out alternative supplier prices before purchasing.

Some companies offer **PRINTERS FOR FREE!** If you sign up to purchasing toner from them. Obviously, their prices can be slightly higher than those of their competitors, but you need to weigh up the overall cost before signing up. For more information visit www.ijtdirect.co.uk. We always recommend that you seek professional advice on purchasing equipment of a technical nature. Speak to the experts!

Mobile telephone and landline telephone

In order for your customers to be able to speak to you, and for you to be able to speak to your suppliers, customers and bank, you will need to make yourself available by telephone, with at least a landline telephone number and also, if possible, a mobile telephone number as well. When first starting your business you could simply use your existing home telephone

number until you become more established, when you may wish to install another line. You may even be profitable enough to have your own office premises!

Getting a mobile 'phone doesn't have to be expensive and it can assist you with your business and enable you to be contacted easily. The mobile telephone industry has expanded rapidly over the last decade and there are great

deals available. It is possible to buy a very modern mobile 'phone for around £50 on a pay as you go tariff. However, a contract arrangement could save you money if your use on pay as you go is high. Therefore, once your business becomes more established, you may

decide to keep the same number but opt for a contract service which you find to be more cost-effective and beneficial to your business. Many providers will offer really good **MOBILES FOR FREE!** If you take out a contract for a set period with a set pricing tariff. You need to do the sums and work out what's best for you, bearing in mind this is a business expense.

INSIDE TIP

Most mobile 'phones are also able to connect to the Internet and email. This is a great way for you to access and check your Internet and email if you don't have immediate access to a laptop or desktop Internet connection. We recommend you obtain a mobile 'phone with this capability as it can be very handy indeed.

We recommend that you speak to the experts before purchasing any broadband, mobile broadband, mobile 'phone or landline to see which is most beneficial to your business needs before committing yourself to any purchase.

YOUR WEBSITE

Getting a website

In this technological age, it is essential that your business has a website on which to market and promote your services. In researching your competitors, you are sure to find that the majority of them have a website to enable their business to be out in the public domain.

Websites are a great way to advertise and market your business as they are essentially a shop window where you

can market and promote your business and services to a wide audience with very little cost.

Many people often think at this point, 'Website... Lots of money? I don't have the skills'. Don't be put off – creating

a website is actually quite simple and inexpensive and you don't need extensive IT skills.

First, your business will need a name before you can create a webpage. You can check if your desired webpage name is available by searching on the Internet for a website domain name checker. Simply enter the desired website address, such as www.mynewbusiness.co.uk or www.mynewbusiness.com, and the domain name checker will then inform you if the required web address is available for you to purchase.

We recommend that you visit a web hosting service which can provide you with a matching web address and email account. In our experience, good web hosting companies can offer a website with several e-mail addresses and web templates for as little as £10 per month.

We have found a good web hosting company to be www.vistaprint.co.uk, who can offer a .co.uk or .com web address with matching email, web template and tools for around £10 per month. The first month is often free and the company will also offer very good rates on printing and stationery for your business. However, there are many other providers who can also undertake this service for you and our best advice is to browse the Internet and find a provider suitable for your business. Having set up your web hosting account, look at competitors' websites to get a feel for your website style and design. We also advise you to keep it simple.

INSIDE TIP

Whilst it might be tempting to approach a complete web solution company to provide the text and layout

of your website, you will find that this is normally quite
expensive. This process is also just as time-consuming
as completing the website yourself, as the web solution
company will normally require all of your details to be
added to the site they are creating anyway. So you
do most of the legwork in providing them with all the
information required on your site!

However, if you are a complete technophobe or don't have
the time, then maybe a web solution company is the right
solution for you, but we recommend that you search the
market and obtain some firm prices. For starting out your
business you will need at least 3 to 5 pages of content with
good photos.

Your website – Homepage

A website will, essentially, be your shop window and will be
your customers' first point of call. Your homepage should be
clear and concise but also punchy and attractive. The idea is
to attract the customer further into your website in order to
market and sell your services and products.

It is important that your homepage describes your business
and services briefly and accurately as search engines will pick
up on your keyword terminology when searching the Internet.

Your homepage should be colourful and exciting with pictures
and text which attract your customers' attention. Make sure
you have some great photos of your stock and equipment
to immediately advertise your products or services to the
customer. Via links on the homepage (e.g. to other websites
and/or organisations you are connected with) you can also
market other/additional products and services.

Website menu

Make your website menu clear and concise to enable potential customers to navigate their way around your site simply and effectively. The menu should be colourful and attractive in order to entice the customer further into your site. For example, attractive words such as 'special offers' or 'exclusive discounts' can often lead people into your site further, as we are all naturally curious and attracted to tempting offers.

INSIDE TIP

Try not to have too many pages attached to your website menu as this will leave visitors confused and make the site difficult to navigate around. As we have said before, keep your website simple, concise and attractive to customers.

Pricing page

Make your pricing strategy clear so that your customer understands how much your products and services cost. If this is not clear, you are unlikely to make a sale and may discourage your customer from browsing your site further.

Make sure that it is clear, if your prices include VAT then say so. For example, if you intend to hire your equipment out for a specific number of hours, this will need to be made clear in the pricing strategy.

We recommend that you have a picture of the product or service you are advertising with the price clearly marked alongside the picture. You can then show that this price

includes or excludes VAT and also outline the number of hours for hire etc.

The following example provides the customer with a clear picture and description of the product, and includes the price and period of work. The customer is immediately aware of your total price and the work period.

**Commercial Office
Cleaning Services**
£10+VAT per hour

On this page you can make the description of the product clear and concise and outline any details or instructions which you feel the customer needs to be aware of. It is wise to have plenty of clear and enticing pictures to enable the customer to understand what the product or service looks like and what they are buying.

Try not to give any false representations or misleading information, as much of your business will be repeat business from customers who like your services and products and who may also recommend you to others.

INSIDE TIP

You can add banners and scrolling text your website by visiting free websites which have banner builders and scrolling text creators FREE. We have found a great banner building site at www.flashvortex.com. This site will enable you to create banners and scrolling text quickly and simply. Your web hosting company should allow you to insert the banner code onto your hosted webpage.

There are many other banner and text creation websites, some of which will charge you for banner scrolling text creators. We have found that the free providers have a simple design and the only downside is that the banner or scrolling text may contain the web provider's website address.

Contact page

This is one of the most important pages on your website as it tells customers where you are located, the area you cover and your contact details, such as your email address, website address, telephone number(s), fax number, etc. Make sure the details on this page are clear and concise as most of your contacts will come from telephone enquiries or email.

It is also wise to have a contact form attached to this page so that potential customers can simply send you a message/query via the Internet which will reach you in the form of an email.

INSIDE TIP

Most website templates will allow you to have a fixed area at the top or bottom of the website pages, giving you the perfect opportunity to ensure that your telephone number and email address is on every single page your potential customer views.

Frequently asked questions (FAQs)

Some websites include a 'frequently asked questions' page. This is useful as customers can refer themselves to this page to find answers to questions that are asked often and can also help customers feel confident when they contact you that the hire is right for them. After all, none of us like to look silly, do we?

On this page you can provide answers to questions such as what area is needed or, how long it takes to complete, your business times, etc., and also dispel any myths associated with the business sector.

These pages are useful when providing answers to customers' questions and you can simply refer customers to this page where the answer to a particular question is explained.

Testimonials Page

Once you are up and running, it is a good idea to ask your customers to provide you with feedback on their experiences with your business. Customers who have enjoyed doing business with you will normally be quite happy to put some kind words in an email or on a comment sheet for you and you can ask them if they are happy for you to place their

comments on your website. You only need a dozen or so comments which can be placed randomly throughout your website – you don't need to include any customer's full details, just the town/city they are from and their surname.

This is a good way of influencing potential customers, as they will read these positive comments, and feel more confident in doing business with you.

Getting your website noticed

Getting traffic to your website is easier than you think. Most search engines will trawl the web for the most appropriate matches to the search criteria typed in the engine. In our experience, one of the most popular search engines is www.google.co.uk. Listing your company with Google is simple, effective and free. Getting your website to the top of the search results is also easier than you think – simply do a bit of research on Google and you will find out how to get your website near the top of a related search.

You should include details of your website and email address on as much of your correspondence and paperwork as possible. In addition to this, there are several areas on the Internet where you can advertise your website for free. For example, Thompson Local www.thomsonlocal.com and Yellow Pages www.yell.com will both allow you to have a free advert both online and in their directories as well.

In addition to these free adverts, you can also gain wider presence online through websites such as www.freeindex.co.uk and many other online advertising sites. We recommend you give these a go as they will cost you nothing.

_____

INSIDE TIP

*Be sure to **read the small print** when placing any adverts on websites to ensure that you do not get charged. There should be no reason for any of the sites to ask for your bank details.*

You will have to be prepared for some follow-up calls from these organisations trying to entice you to advertise and sign up for more expensive campaigns. In our experience the free ads should be enough. However, if you wish to expand your marketing campaign, you can always take these organisations up on their offer. If you wish to retain your free advert, simply politely declined their offers.

YOUR BUSINESS'S PHYSICAL IMAGE

In addition to the technical aspects of business today, there still remain the good, old fashioned, tried and tested, business methods, such as the physical image of your business to the customer/clients, whether it be your shop front or your vehicle.

The image you portray to your potential customers or clients is one of the most important issues for your business. A smart, clean and professional looking company does better than a scruffy, dirty and unprofessional looking one.

Business cards and stationery – Get free business cards!

Clearly, the old-fashioned, tried and tested method of marketing is to ensure that you have a matching set of

stationery. This will include a letterhead that matches your website, a set of matching business cards, invoices, 'With Compliments' slips, etc. Having well presented business stationery presents a professional and image conscious company which will give your customers confidence in the company they are hiring. Get your free business cards here: www.vistaprint.co.uk

Getting your company logo

Some companies decide to have a logo or brand portraying their business and we recommend that you consider having a business logo which represents your business. This not only looks professional but it also helps your business to be immediately recognised in the local area.

Both the stationery and the logo needn't cost the earth. A business logo can be created by simply using Microsoft Word or a clipart package from your local PC World or Internet software provider. However, you will find that www.vistaprint.co.uk have a range of logos that can be purchased in varying forms at very little cost. This will often include a colour and black-and-white version in differing forms such as JPEG's or PDF files. These can then be added to your stationery Word documents website and any files you wish to produce.

Company Uniform

Dependent upon the business that you are starting, it may be beneficial to have company branded clothing. Whatever your business and whether it is office based or site based, it

can be beneficial and present a professional image to have a branded uniform, or some form of recognisable clothing, that instantly links an individual back to your business.

Even if your business requires you to wear personal protective equipment such as a hard hat or overalls, there is no reason why your company logo cannot be incorporated into your work wear.

Company branded clothing is often inexpensive and does two important things. First, it creates a professional image to your customers and clients as well as identifying your staff or yourself as a member of the business. Secondly, it also provides a very inexpensive method of advertising. For example, when having your T-shirts or overalls produced, for a very small additional cost you can often have your website email address and telephone number(s) added, say, to the breast pocket or back.

Professional Organisations

Being a member of a professional organisation can also help your business too. You are telling your customers that you are serious about what you do and that standards mean a lot to your company.

Cleaning Support Services Association

The CSSA is well known in the UK for the support and events that it often hosts. You are advised to attend these events  if you can. They offer opportunities and contacts. They also offer a member area where clients can choose from their list of

contractors to tender for contracts. This could be invaluable to your business. If you wish to join, you will need to be vetted by the association in order to meet it's requirements.

Your membership can come with benefits by getting cheaper insurance and fleet deals by being a member. You can also use the logo on your stationary and vehicles, which helps you business look professional and organised.

National Carpet Cleaning Association

For those wishing to expand into this area, the industry is well supported by this association. Advice and support  for your business can be gained from joining or contacting the association. This can be from client leads right down to where to get the best machines and chemicals from. They offer comprehensive training on all types of cleaning methods.

If you are considering offering these services, please do get in touch with any one of the organisations that cover this area. They will only be too pleased to help. Their technical help line is good and they also run a sponsor scheme.

Federation of Window Cleaners

You may also be undertaking or expanding by offering window cleaning services as part of you company's work portfolio. This federation will have lots of support and advice on how to offer these services and best practice.

They have been established since 1947 and offer training and support to its members that offer these services. Again the

logo can be used for business purposes all the time you are a member.

UK Cleaning Products Industry Association

This association provide a slightly differing service from the rest. They can be invaluable to your business. Support on all types of cleaning  products and the methods used to clean can be found. They employ experts who can advise on the cleaning regulations and legislation related to cleaning products and associated chemicals etc. used in products. More recently they offer advice and support on green cleaning which is becoming more popular with the larger clients. Mainly due to their environmental policy requirements and corporate responsibility to the environment.

Take a look at their web pages and glean what you can to se if you feel it is worthwhile being a member.

HEALTH AND SAFETY

Health & Safety should be a key consideration in the early stages of setting up your business. The Health & Safety Executive (HSE) are the key organisation, along with the Local Authority, who may have an interest in the safe operation of your business.

Before you start trading you must make yourself aware of all the requirements of running a business and the health and safety elements attached to it. The HSE offer some really good advice as well as leaflets and online resources to help you stay on the right side of the law.

The HSE leaflet 'An Introduction to Health and Safety in Small Businesses' INDG259 ISBN 978 0 7176 2685 4 is a good place to start and this can be obtained at HSE Books www.hsebooks.co.uk / Tel. No. 01787 881165. The subject is vast and cannot be covered in detail in the publication.

INSIDE TIP

Register your business with the HSE and partner in any local schemes. A safe business is a good business as far as customers and clients are concerned. We also recommend you discuss this area with an appropriately qualified health and safety practitioner. You can find a qualified health and safety specialist at the Institute of Occupational Safety and Health (IOSH) www.iosh.co.uk / Tel. No. 0116 257 3100.

CHAPTER 3

Cleaning Services

TYPES OF SERVICES OFFERED & TYPICAL CHARGES

The one-off clean – Through word of mouth or advertising

This can be where a householder wishes to simply spruce up and tidy their home or a business who wishes to spruce up a new premises. Alternatively, it could be that call to get them out of trouble, from burst pies to blocked drains. These are often a good way for you to market your business and can often end up in repeat work. Be sure to undertake a thorough job, and make sure that you meet the customer's requirements.

The one-off can range from a simple one off task to a large one off contract of a large retail premises. These are also a great marketing tool for you to obtain business from having a great portfolio of work to show potential clients or to include in tenders. Be sure to show all new customers your portfolio of work.

When undertaking this work, you should leave a signboard on the premises for a few days, as part of your service. Free advertising is too good an opportunity to miss.

 how2become

One off's may mean sub contracting for another cleaning contractor. Don't be put off by this as making contacts with larger companies can only do your business good.

Regular & Scheduled Cleaning

This is a good way to earn a regular income stream to underpin the other areas of work within your business and will help cash flow. Many companies or customers will require regular cleaning on a cyclical basis. For example, a restaurant will need to keep its front of house and kitchen clean and tidy to entice customers in. Why not fix your prices and book them in for regular cleaning services.

Alternatively, you may have local pubs or restaurants that require regular work every other year, in kitchen deep cleans etc. Keeping touch with these clients by way of a Christmas card or invite to events, is a good way of keeping regular work.

This is a great way of ensuring your business turns over a consistent and regular income stream. You will often find that customers will on occasion, ask you to quote and complete some extra work that they require. In addition to this, you will also find that many customers will ask you to return the following year to undertake some more work. This work also offers you the opportunity to undertake extra services such as window cleaning, or duct cleaning for example (if you intend to offer this).

There is also the possibility of undertaking larger contracts such as cyclical cleaning contracts for housing associations or local authorities. You can approach your local authority or other organisations within your area and offer your services

to corporate clients. However, you must bear in mind the capabilities of the company as undertaking large areas will require larger industrial equipment to enable you to undertake this work effectively.

Insurance Work

This is another area of work for which your business may wish to undertake. Many insurance companies or loss adjusters have lists of cleaning contractors to deal with claims. This spans across the domestic and commercial market. From serious fire damage to wind and impact damage.

Getting on an insurers list of approved contractors will definitely improve your chances of winning work or being invited to tender. Search the internet or make a few calls to see if it is possible to get onto an approved list. You may have to sometimes persist with this, but polite nudging in the right direction can pay dividends later on.

Approved Cleaning Contractor Lists

These can often be worth while. Getting your company on an approved list of contractors often improve your chances of success for winning work. It is therefore worth while looking into individual lists for companies and organisations where possible. Some on line portals offer this, but be wary of paying for these services.

You will need to submit paper work to each and every body that has their own list and we must warn you that some ask for a lot of information. In some instances it can be a complete waste of time, in others it can be very fruitful. It will be a case of deciding what's best for you and your company on whether to apply for these lists.

HOW TO PRICE A CLEANING CONTRACT

Before you enter the market place you need to be aware of the way in which to price. Especially for those commercial buildings as you may price it wrong and loose money. This would not be great for your business or reputation.

Establish a floor rate: You will need to establish a price per square meter or per square foot. This will depend on how your client's like to work. Although metric areas are now used a lot, many companies' still use feet, so you need to do both.

Arrange a walk-through of a potential client business to assess the cleaning needs. Some companies may only want rubbish removal and vacuuming, whereas another business may require a lot more.

There are a lot of tried and tested methods to help you price contracts. For example, you can charge a standard price of per square foot/meter. You will need to ask the client for information regarding the office square footage/meterage. Then you will need to check this on site to ensure that it is accurate. Not forgetting those hidden areas. Digital laser measures are a great tool. But make sure you get an expensive and accurate model, as you don't want to get this wrong.

Establish a time charge: For some clients you can simply charge an hourly rate, this is popular with domestic clients, as it is simple and effective. Walk through the property and estimate how long it will take to clean the office or home and price accordingly. Consider the amount of carpet/ hard flooring, plus any desks, offices, bathrooms and glass surfaces. Don't forget to ensure your customer knows what you are including and excluding in this contracted rate.

Discounted Rates: For those larger regular clients you may apply a discounted rate for cleaning depending on the frequency required. Offices cleaned more often will be less dirty and take less time to clean so it should be a win win situation for you. Be sure to make your terms of business clear as these clients will need to be good payers for you to offer discounted rates. Be sure to make it clear that this rate is offered as long as payment is kept to the terms of business for your company.

Extra services: Be sure to include additional services in any cleaning tender or bid. If you offer window cleaning for example or carpet cleaning services, make sure you outline this. Many companies vary, and some may request services outside your basic package. For example, basic packages may include dusting, sweeping, mopping, vacuuming and rubbish removal. Complete a menu of services offered outside those services requested and include this on your web pages.

Be sure to consider the following services for which you can target customers:

- Student houses – end of term cleans
- House rental cleans
- House move cleans
- Office and House one off's
- House clearance cleans
- Deep office cleans
- Care home contracts
- Hotel contracts

- Golf clubs & other club premises
- Night cleans
- Special security clearance cleans (security clear your staff)

Create a leads database: Use or create a program that allows you to enter fields such as dates, addresses, telephone numbers, contact names and notes for contact history. Excel is great for this purpose. Populate your database with information from companies that meet your criteria, such as building of a certain size or in a location within your proposed service area. Make sure you contact these customers regularly with e-mails or phone calls, but not to hard.

Referral discounts: Don't forget to ask all of your existing customers to recommend you. Offer them a rebate for any successful leads that come through. That way they have a vested interest to get you new customers.

QUOTING & TENDERING FOR WORK – METHODS & TIPS

Now that you have established how to price a cleaning contract, you need to win business. To do this, you will need to submit quotations estimates or tenders to your customers. For the domestic market you may only need to respond to your customers by submitting a quotation or an estimate for their consideration. However, it is more common in the commercial market for you to be required to submit a tender. This may be a tender submission directly to the customer or as a subcontractor to a larger organisation who may well be a main contractor submitting a tender to win work.

Estimates

An estimate is exactly as it says, an estimation of the time equipment and materials required to undertake work for your customer. Whilst an estimate is exactly that, you should try and keep your estimation as close to your final charges as possible. The last thing you would wish is for your business to obtain a bad reputation of estimating low and charging high. Your customers and clients would normally expect your estimate not to exceed around 10% over what was originally estimated. Unless of course, the client has asked for something completely different following your initial meeting, in which case, they should be treated as extras and priced as such.

When undertaking your estimate you should ensure that you obtain and interpret the customer's requirements exactly. If you are in any doubt of what it is the client is asking for, you should request clarification in order that you get your estimate right. This shows that you have listened to your customer and will stand you in good stead when you return your estimates for consideration. It is also good practice to turn your estimates around in a fairly short space of time. This shows your commitment to the customer and demonstrates that your business is efficient and responsive.

It should be clear on your estimate of what work is required and a breakdown of your charges in order that the customer can consider your estimate easily. Whilst these do not have to outline of all your materials, approximate time and materials will normally suffice.

When visiting customer's premises, it is good practice to ensure that you are presented well. Believe it or not, you

can look too smart! For example, turning up in an expensive car and a designer suit will convince your customer that you are expensive and making too much money. Instead, it is better to turn up in a clean vehicle which should be preferably sign written. In addition to this, you should either wear your company uniform or dress smart but relatively casual.

Some customers may take time to arrange their finances and make arrangements for the work to be undertaken. A polite phone call a couple of weeks after your estimate has been submitted, in order to follow up, would not be unwelcome. Just because a customer has not contacted you it does not mean they are not considering you for the work. Be sure to offer a discount price for ordering within a set period. It is also wise to ensure that your estimate is clear on how long your price lasts. For example, it is not uncommon for cleaning contractors to hold their prices for 6 to 8 weeks and some even up to 3 months. Remember, even if the work requested is a small amount, it can often lead to larger value works and in difficult times, small clients can be the ones that keep you in business!

Quotations

Quotations differ from estimates as they are a *fixed* sum for the work required by the client and you are required to undertake the work outlined in your quotation for the amount stated.

Make no mistake, with a quotation; your customer will expect you to deliver the cleaning services outlined in your quotation for the exact amount that you have priced. Some

clients prefer quotations as opposed to estimates, so that they are fully aware of the extent of costs of your services and have a clear understanding of their financial risks. You should ensure that you get your quotation right, at it as it is imperative that you do not lose money on quoting the job which will cost you more to undertake.

As with estimates, you should ensure that the quotation has an expiry period in order that you are not exposed to risk of rising prices over time. Although, you may wish to outline in your covering letter, that in some circumstances you may stand by your prices over your exclusion period. Just do a quick check to ensure that your quotation still stands and you're happy to undertake the work for the price quoted.

The same ethos applies to undertake quotations for customers, as submitting estimates, as it best to ensure that you turn your information around quickly and that is clear and concise and that you take the advice given with regard to making sure you are smart and effective in your visit to the customer.

You can be rest assured, that the manner in which you undertake your estimates and quotations, will often stand you in good stead for undertaking the work. For example, small things such as wiping your shoes when entering a customers house or office premises can make all the difference. If they offer a drink, politely accept. It's those little things that attract the customer or client to you undertaking the work. Customers like to think that you will respect and look after their premises when you're working there. Signals given by your polite behaviour can often mean the difference between winning and losing a job!

Customer service is very important to people these days. Customers are often looking for that extra assurance. People are living extremely busy and time-consuming lives much like us, so they are looking for that piece of mind.

Extras whilst on the job

These are works which you may be asked to price whilst you are working at your customer's home or office. For example, you may have been asked to undertake particular services in the quotation or estimate and once on site your client or customer asks you to undertake more work over and above what you originally priced. It is often good practice to agree what is required on site and treat it as a separate piece of work. Either provide a quotation or estimate on a quick turnaround. Some contractors carry a small carbon copy estimate book, so you can provide instant quotes or estimates!

This ensures that your customers are aware of the cost of such extras and are given the opportunity to question or accept your quotations or estimates for the extra work. This approach avoids any confusion or dispute over your final bill. Many contractors provide acceptance forms at the back of the quote or estimate, so that the customer can simply sign a carbon copy for your records. Effectively turning your quote or estimate into an instant order. This will constitute the basis of an agreement between you and the customer of undertaking the work for the price given, and should any disagreement arise you are in a better position to request your money.

Tendering cleaning contracts

Tendering for work or a project is in a different arena from quoting or estimating work. Tenders are essentially a more formal estimate or quotation of work. These are normally required by professional bodies or organisations, in order that they can fill their procurement rules and requirements. Tenders would normally be required by the Larger corporate organisations such as government departments or charities which need to demonstrate value for money to their members, stakeholders or managers. Particularly, where the work value is in larger volumes.

The way in which you present your quotations or estimates may not be acceptable for a tender. You will normally see that the tender documentation that you are sent will be quite specific in the information for which it asks. You should pay particular attention to completing the tender information exactly as requested. For example, it is not uncommon for tenders to be rejected if they are not submitted on time or in the correct format. Often tenders will need to be sealed and labelled in a particular format or submitted to a secure electronic mail inbox. You should pay particular attention to the method in which your tender should be submitted. You should ensure that you comply with the tender documentation as much as possible.

If you cannot comply with the tender documentation in its full form, there is normally little point in applying. You will be wasting your own and your staff's time in submitting a price which does not comply with the tender. Should you need any clarification or wish to submit information which does not strictly comply with the tender documentation you

are advised to seek guidance from the tendering company in order that they are happy for you to deviate from the tender specification.

Some of the mistakes made by businesses pricing for work in a tender environment is creating the right image to the client. For example, the client will normally be aware of your need to visit the premises or site to which the tender relates. When visiting the site, it is crucial to get your timing right. You should ensure that you visit the site in the early or mid-point in the tender period. Visiting this site very close to the tender deadline shows that you have rushed to the tender document as you would have only visited site days or in some cases hours before the tender was due. This does not paint a very organised picture of your company. Avoiding this is very simple, visit the site early and show an early interest in the tender by taking plenty of photographs or maybe even a video of the area for which the tender relates. This will enable you to revisit your site visit at any time in the future.

Delivering the tenders by hand and is often cheaper and ensures that you can physically confirm that the tender has been handed in. Try to obtain a time and dated receipt from the point of delivery. You will find that some companies operate this procedure anyway, and will provide you with a tender receipt as part of their normal practices.

If you are using the services of a courier, you need to ensure that the courier physically hands the document to a receptionist or member of staff where the tender is to be received. It is not uncommon for unreliable couriers to simply leave the document and go about their business. The best way to avoid this is to use a courier service which you know

and trust to deliver your documents on time and also in a manner in which it is expected to be delivered. It is often good practice to ensure that you have a delivery contract with your courier as failure to deliver your tender documentation correctly can result in your business losing work.

Subcontracting cleaning services for a larger company

If you are subcontracting for a larger cleaning contractor and your price is required to form part of their tender. You should certainly ask your client (the main contractor) how they wish for the information to be presented. It is also good practice to have sight of the tender document which is being passed to the main contractor. In some circumstances, main contractors will seek advice from you in order to fulfil the requirements of the tender.

It is not uncommon in some circumstances, for the main contractor to come back after winning the work and offer you your sub contract, on the basis of a discount applied to your original price. Beware, if you are prepared to accept a discounted offer on your original price you are sending a message to the main contractor that you are willing to drop your prices in order to secure work. The decision on whether to do this, will purely be your own, and your need to weigh up the pros and cons of doing so.

Term cleaning contracts or cleaning frameworks

If your business is really doing well and expanding, you may wish to secure work with corporate blue chip clients or local authorities and housing associations etc. Many of these

organisations will have large capital and revenue spends and can been a good source of regular income.

You will often find that many of these organisations operate typical contracts on a term contract basis or operate from frameworks of cleaning contractors or cleaning suppliers. In order to secure work of this nature you will need to be adequately insured to fill the requirements of such organisations. Most corporate clients which will need you to be well organised and well established. These types of clients will expect you to have the appropriate health and safety mechanisms and safety frameworks in place as well as systems and procedures alongside a financial stability. This is a very specialist area and more guidance is given on this subject in our products. Please feel free to visit our web shop and purchase further guides to help you succeed in this area.

TYPICAL EQUIPMENT REQUIRED

Personal protection

As with any work activity, personal protective equipment (PPE) is paramount and required by law if you are operating as a business. Below are examples of typical and very useful, combined pieces of PPE, designed specifically to protect you conforming to all the necessary 'CE and 'EN' standards.

Dust mask or respirator for protection from paint fumes & dust
£8-25

Purpose made overalls or disposable paper coveralls
£3-35

Safety glasses for eye protection
£4-16

Work gloves or rubber gloves for hand protection
£3-8

Knee pad protection for kneeling work
£8-18

High visibility vest or jacket for visibility safety (required on some industrial sites)
£3-90 – £55

Essential & well equipped health & safety first aid kit
£33-49

Emergency eye wash kit
£12-44

Spill kit to minimise any damage from cleaning chemical spills
£10-30

Large dust sheets for protection and clearing up
£13-35 each

Typical cleaning machinery & equipment

Below you will find machinery and equipment that is used in both commercial and domestic cleaning. Some of which can be hired rather than purchased, in order to get your business off the ground.

Upright or trailing vacuum cleaners are used in both commercial and domestic settings. These can range **from £100-400** for a good quality heavy duty vacuum cleaner.

Industrial carpet cleaners for those deep cleans or for insurance works. These can vary in price and are available in semi commercial or fully commercial versions. You will need to decide what to invest into. Consideration needs to be given to the investment return if purchasing. Staff will also require training in use and the chemicals required to use the machines.

Costs range **between £400 and £4000** for a more commercial machine. These can be hired **from £29 per day** from most local hire companies. Such as HSS www.hss.com.

The typical cleaning trolley required for those larger commercial premises. These can be stored on site if a regular cleaning contract is won. They vary in quality and price. However, we recommend that you invest in a good commercial version to ensure that it lasts. These get used a lot and will help to speed contracts up if equipped correctly. Prices range **from £30 to £300** for the more commercial versions.

Good quality professional jet washers are also a good investment, if you are offering services such as patio/pavement cleaning. These can be purchased at a reasonable price and the petrol versions can be used anywhere. Electrical versions can also be used and are cheaper to purchase. Staff will also need to be trained in use and operation. These range in price **from £200 to £2000** for the more robust commercial system.

Floor buffers or floor scrubbers. These can be from hand operated to complete vehicles for those larger spaces such as airports. You will again need to decide on whether these are for your business or not as they will need to pay for themselves. Staff will also need to be fully trained. These can range **from £400 – £5000** dependant on the size required.

These can also be hired starting **from £23 to 250 per day** for ride on versions. Some machines have dual capability to scrub, buff and wash.

Consumables

These are a major part of the business sector and will be stock items for your business, such as bleach, polish, chemicals, pads, dusters etc. So you need to ensure that these are good enough to make the job easy, but not too expensive.

Make sure you get a good stockist/supplier as you really do not want to carry too much stock. Just in time ordering will work if you get a reasonable supplier keeping your costs down.

Try companies such as:

www.nexuscleaningsupplies.co.uk
www.onestopcleaningsupplies.co.uk

Tools & equipment generally

Much of this equipment will depend on the type of work that you pick up. Remember, these are business assets so any purchases will be off set against your profit and loss accounts. Plus if you are VAT registered, this can be claimed back later in the financial year. Whilst we cannot give you an exhaustive list of tools and equipment required, here are some more common items used by cleaning contractors.

Professional step ladder 6-8ft £45-100

A must, is a good sturdy step ladder with large treads with anti-slip plastic insert of the folding steel steps provide comfortable safe access to higher areas. Can be used as steps with a convenient safety handrail or a stool with backrest. Slim and compact when folded for easy storage.
£30-200

Hop up platform – £25-45

For high usage, this will become one of your most useful tools on the job, so ensure you get a good quality and brand to ensure longevity. Available from www.machinemart. co.uk or www.screwfix.co.uk plus many other popular tool outlets.

Professional extension work ladder 2/3 section – £120-350

Again, how often do you see a window cleaner without a ladder? Ensure that you have a good quality and robust ladder. These should be regularly maintained and kept in good working order. A good ladder will last you a long time and will be used daily.

Professional ladder accessories – £ varies dependant on selection

Ladder accessories are also very popular with this type of work, ladder off stands and ladder hooks for example, normally form part of the every day routine. It is also wise to have a decent set of ladder clamps that can be locked when fixed to your vehicle.

Residual Current Device (RCD) or Power Transformer – £10-75

You should not operate or use any electrical equipment without the use of a residual current device (RCD) or a transformer to covert power to a safe working level for each piece of electrical equipment used.

Most commercial sites will not permit you to work without a transformer. These are very small and will enable you to operate your electrical equipment **safely**. You simply plug the RCD or the transformer directly into the mains socket outlet and then plug your electrical equipment into the front of the RCD or transformer. It is essential that these are PAT tested to ensure safe operation.

Extension Cable Reel

You will need an extension lead or cable reel. We recommend that you get a reel as they are easier to pack away, store and transport as well as being easier to use. The cable should be at least 30 metres long, as anything shorter could lead to problems when connecting your equipment. You can buy cable reels up to 50 metres long. We recommend that you undertake a PAT test to ensure any extension lead or cable is safe to use, even if it is new and unused.

We recommend that you look at your local tool trade suppliers or search the net for distribution based professional suppliers. There is a massive range of suppliers for tools in this trade and bargains can be sought if you look!

PROTECTING YOUR EQUIPMENT

Mark your equipment

Cleaning tools and machinery are expensive pieces of equipment and, unfortunately, may be stolen, only to be resold or used to your detriment. As with any expensive piece of equipment, it is wise to mark it with your company name and telephone number to ensure that, if it is lost or stolen, identification is easy and you may even get it returned to you. We recommend that you mark your equipment in an obscure place known only to you. You should also ensure that you have a complete list of your entire stock, not only as a record for insurance purposes, but also so that you know exactly how much equipment you have and its value.

Storing your equipment

Your equipment should be stored in a safe, dry and secure environment. Try not to leave your machinery or associated equipment in your vehicle over night as you may attract criminal activity. If this is not really practical you will need to store your equipment securely. Lock boxes for tools are quite common such as a van vault; these are securely bolted to the chassis of the vehicle:

If you are just starting up your business, a secure garage would be suitable for storing a small amount of equipment,

but check that you are permitted to operate from home? Always check with your local planning authority regarding working from home and using your premises as a base for business activity.

Try not to store your tools directly on the ground as moisture may penetrate into the equipment and affect its life expectancy. It is a good idea to store them on a wall, enabling them to be stored off the ground and ensuring ventilation beneath them. This would also keep your equipment dry should there be an accidental spillage onto the ground.

Good and clear access is important so you will need to ensure that you have plenty of room to manoeuvre around, and lift, all of your equipment easily. During winter months it is also essential that you have adequate lighting in order to see what you're doing when storing and packing away materials.

Remember, keep your costs down and only use as much storage as necessary. As the business grows, you can expand or rent more space.

If you are starting out and do not have sufficient space to store your equipment, you could investigate the possibility of renting one of the widely available storage units which are often open 7 days a week from very early to very late in the day. This will enable you to get your business off the ground until you are able to operate from your own premises or storage facility. You will need to ensure that your equipment is fully insured against theft or damage if you intend to leave equipment in someone else's premises as you will often find that commercial storage companies will not insure your individual equipment without paying an additional fee on your rental.

Insuring your equipment

You should certainly think about insuring your equipment against theft and malicious damage. You will need to weigh up the cost and benefit of insurance as it can often be expensive and we recommend that you shop around to obtain several quotes before committing yourself to a policy.

Buying Materials for the business

One of the other important parts of running a cleaning business is the purchase of materials. We covered earlier in this guide, the use of supplier accounts, but what will be your typical material purchases?

Much of the materials purchased for jobs will be required from the outset and may need to be stored by you whilst the work progresses. Only you will know what brands of materials and supplies you like to work with.

Clearly what you use may also affect the price that the can complete the work for. However, if you like to work with a particular brand of supplier for example, it may be more expensive to buy. But, if you are familiar the time saved in using this brand may well offset the increased price so the cost of the undertaking the work may be the same or less.

Find what suits you and try and use regular brands and materials that you are familiar with. These should be purchased from a trade supplier where most branches will stock the required materials on the shelf in large quantities. It is not uncommon for companies to ask for payment of materials at the start of the job on domestic work. However, the commercial market is different and much of the materials will have to be invoiced and many client companies will be

on 30-90 day payment terms to you, so bear this in mind when pricing large works.

CHAPTER 4

Running the business

INDEMNITY INSURANCES

Public Liability Insurance (PI)

One of the key elements of running any business is to ensure that you have adequate and sufficient public liability insurance. Most insurers recommend that you have a minimum level of cover of £1 million. However, you may wish to obtain more cover for your business dependent upon the level of risk which you feel is acceptable.

The insurance is relatively cheap and there are many providers who can cover your business needs for small premium. Most of these premiums are based on the type and level of activity of your business. Insurers will be interested in your turnover and where your business is undertaken, e.g. at a licensed premise such as a public house or hotel.

Most customers will want to be reassured that you have adequate insurance cover and this will also help in marketing your business as a responsible and professional organisation.

So what does PI cover do?

Public liability insurance will cover any award of damages given to a member of public as result of injury to their person or damage to their property which is deemed to be caused by you or your company. Most insurers will also cover legal fees and also costs and expenses for hospital treatment which the NHS may claim from your business.

It is imperative that you talk to a professional insurance adviser in relation to obtaining public liability insurance as there any many exclusions and warranties that can be applied to your public liability policy. Talking to a professional insurance adviser will ensure that your insurance cover meets your business needs and also ensure that you are adequately covered. We recommend that you find a broker from the British Insurance Brokers Association (BIBA) and that you search the Internet for like-for-like quotes. When doing so, you will need to look at the small print to ensure that what you are purchasing is adequate.

INSIDE TIP

*Make sure that you **read the small print**. Speak to a professional and make sure that you complete all paperwork clearly and accurately to ensure that, in the event of a claim, you are fully covered. Also, if you are hiring staff, don't forget employer's liability insurance.*

Disclaimer

You will need to create your own disclaimer. Sample disclaimers are readily available from the Internet and are

often provided free of charge from the manufacturers and suppliers of major equipment.

Your customers should sign a copy of your disclaimer. These can be printed on the rear of your order form, one of which is left with the customer and the other retained by you for office purposes and to ensure that your records are up-to-date.

INSIDE TIP

Ask professional organisations for a free example of a disclaimer which you can then adapt and use to suit your business. We recommend that you get advice from an expert when creating or customising your disclaimer to ensure that you have created a document that benefits you and your business.

KEEPING RECORDS

Keeping records is a key part of running a business and you will need to keep accurate records. You will need to be organised and have effective filing systems to enable your business to operate correctly, easily and efficiently. Your accountant or bookkeeper will need you to provide them with these records so that your accounts can be organised, recorded and audited. Outside bodies may also need to inspect your records and having them to hand and organised will present a much more professional image.

Providing Receipts: You will need to provide your customers with receipts for any sales. It is a good idea to keep a receipt book or buy software that provides you with this facility. Some

providers offer this for free. You will need to test the market to find a suitable method that suits your business.

Keeping Receipts: You should retain receipts for *everything* you buy which is related to your business. These will be required by your accountant or book keeper so that your business expenses can be recorded and offset against your profit.

Packing slips: If you are sending items to your customers by post or courier, then you will need to enclose a packing slip telling them, what was ordered and the unit numbers along with the price.

Providing Invoices: It will be necessary for you to provide some customers with an invoice so that they can pay you through their own company. Providing invoices is simple and you can design your own invoices with the required fields or, alternatively, you can purchase some software or search the Internet for a free invoice pro forma.

Keeping Invoices: You will need to keep all invoices in order as a record what you have billed and what has been paid against your business income. Your bookkeeper or accountant will require you to keep copies of all invoices and credit notes which you issue or receive.

Credit Notes: You may need to issue a credit note if, for instance, a customer has been overcharged or as a refund for goods or services. You should keep a copy of all credit notes so that your accountant or book keeper can include them in the business accounts. Providing a credit note is simple and you can design your own credit note with the required fields

or, alternatively, you can purchase some software or search the Internet for a free credit note pro forma.

Statements: In addition to all the other paperwork, statements will be a frequent piece of record-keeping you will receive. Not only will your bank provide you with regular statements (electronically or in paper form), but your suppliers will often provide you with a statement of account so that you can see what you owe them and when you need to pay them.

You should always review your statements in great detail to ensure that they are accurate and so that you can keep an eye on the activity through your business and your business account. This is also essential if you have staff or are aware of fraudulent activity that may affect your business. Don't be afraid to question your statements to ensure that they are factually correct.

Daily Inspection/Records: Regular daily inspection will ensure that all your equipment remains in a good and safe condition to enable your customers to have an uninterrupted service from you. This will not only ensure that your equipment remains in a safe condition but also make you aware of any repairs or any major work that needs to be undertaken.

Your manufacturer or supplier will be able to give you advice on inspecting and maintaining the equipment you have bought from them and you should follow the manufacturer's advice and guidance.

INSIDE TIP
Suppliers and manufacturers will often have examples of daily inspection record sheets for you to adapt and

use for your business. When purchasing your equipment, make sure you ask them if they can provide you with a template which you can adapt to suit your business.

Risk Assessments/Health & Safety records: Risk assessments and health and safety records are a fundamental requirement for all businesses. In order to operate within the law, all UK businesses will have a range of risk assessments and records to maintain. You should retain copies of your risk assessments and health and safety records and review them regularly.

All employers must look at and record all work activities that could cause harm to their staff, their visitors or the public in order to ascertain whether they are doing enough to meet their legal obligations. In doing this within your business sector, you are recognizing and documenting the risks and working practices and how you can deal with them in a safe manner.

It is important that reviews are carried out systematically and all foreseeable risks are considered and documented. The level of detail recorded should relate to the level of risk your business activities pose. We recommend that you seek professional advice from an appropriately qualified health and safety practitioner. More information can be found at www.hse.gov.uk, where lots of useful tips and information can be found both online and in hard copy.

Portable Appliance Testing (PAT): Portable appliance testing is commonplace in today's business world. Good advice can be sought from www.hse.gov.uk. There are some myths around this subject, so you should check before you spend and also get professional advice. You should ensure that all

electrical equipment is in a serviceable and safe condition. This is usually done by carrying out a visual and mechanical test known as a PAT test. You should keep all PAT test records and ensure that they are renewed once they have expired.

Here is a list of actions suggested by the HSE:

- Check that electrical equipment is suitable for the work and way in which it is going to be used.

- Check that electrical equipment is in good condition.

- Check that equipment is suitable for the electrical supply with which it is going to be used, and the electrical supply is safe.

- It is often beneficial to use a Residual Current Device (RCD) between the electrical supply and the equipment.

- Make sure that the user of the equipment is trained to use it safely and can keep others safe.

- Make sure the user knows what personal protective equipment to wear, how to use it, and make sure that they do.

Equipment should be physically capable of doing the job and designed and constructed so that mechanical and electrical stresses do not cause the equipment to become unsafe. All records and instructions on use should be kept for your reference or training of your staff/customers.

Additional regular inspections may be required where a risk assessment indicates this is necessary and you should also keep records of these.

INSIDE TIP

Contrary to common belief, not all equipment requires an annual inspection. Hired equipment will clearly need checking more frequently than, say, the office lamp. We recommend that you contact the HSE as they have some really good advice and information, both online and on the telephone.

Testing and certification: All new equipment should come with full certification. However, will need to ensure your equipment is tested and certified annually in order for it to be used safely. Failure to do so could result in a claim or cause your insurance to be invalid.

Collecting and managing data: By keeping e-mail addresses, telephone numbers and business addresses, etc., you will be able to build a database in an Excel spreadsheet or in your email contacts. This information is then available so that you can include all, or some, of these customers or suppliers in any future mail shot or marketing/launch event.

A good customer database will add value to your business should you wish to sell or help to attract investors as you will be able to provide evidence of the number of customers you have attached to your business. A database of your preferred stockists and suppliers will also be useful in ensuring that your supply chain is maintained.

You should ensure that all data you retain complies with the Data Protection Act and any other associated legislation connected to keeping people's personal details and the sharing of information. We highly recommend that you

carry out research and talk to an expert in this area to ensure that you are not breaching any associated legislation when retaining people's personal details. You should also ensure that details of customers and suppliers are disposed of in a safe and correct manner. These details should be destroyed so that they are illegible. You can achieve this with either a good cross cut paper shredder or by disposing of the details using a data safe disposal company.

INSIDE TIP

Ensure that you back up and save all of your contacts on a separate computer, disk, CD or memory stick to ensure that valuable data is not lost. Don't forget, you could lose hours and hours of work if you fail to back up or take spare copies of your digital information. We recommend that you take professional advice on saving and backing up all data and information relating to your business. This can often be done cheaper than you think and will certainly help you out in the event of a data crisis!

INSIDE TIP

When visiting the industry's trade fairs or shows, you can often pick up free memory sticks which businesses use to promote their products or services. Use this free resource – it is not uncommon for suppliers or manufacturers to give away memory sticks with up to 2 or 3 gigabytes of memory.

TRANSPORT

Transport and getting around

Many of you may have seen large vans or Lorries with company's logos or adverts all over the sides of the vehicles. These are normally the larger providers in your area.

However, when starting out you will not need to go out and spend thousands of pounds purchasing a new van or lorry to undertake your business. A second-hand goods van that is fit for purpose will do. Remember to check out the vehicle's history and ensure that all good practice and advice is followed when purchasing. A good site for vehicle sales is www.autotrader.co.uk where there are thousands of vehicles for sale.

Ensure that your vehicle is thoroughly inspected and that you get the best vehicle for the budget. It's best to take a friend or mechanic to ensure that you have a good opportunity to inspect the vehicle fully. Be sure to follow all good advice. Both the RAC and the AA have good advice that can be followed when buying a second-hand or new vehicle. Alternatively, for a fee, you can use either of these organisations to inspect your vehicle.

You are also advised to undertake a car data check to confirm the details of the vehicle. This often comes with an insurance backed guarantee. Whilst a car data check may be expensive, it is money well spent and ensures that you know more about the vehicle you are purchasing.

Find more information at www.hpicheck.com, www.theaa.com or www.rac.co.uk.

Buying a vehicle at auction: Buying a vehicle at auction is often a popular way of obtaining a cheap vehicle at a good price. However, auctions are not for the fainthearted and you should be experienced before you attend any auction and ensure that you know what you are doing. Advice on buying at auction and a list of auction events can be found at www.british-car-auctions.co.uk.

We recommend that you always speak to an expert when purchasing any kind of vehicle to ensure that you do not make any expensive mistakes.

Alternative transport for your business

If you are just starting up your business and you do not have the capital to purchase a new vehicle, there are alternatives. If you have a small amount of equipment, you can purchase a box trailer. Most small box trailers can be  towed by the average family car and all you will need to ensure is that your car has the necessary towing capacity for the trailer you wish to purchase. It is also a good idea to ensure that you have some experience of towing. A well established and good trailer manufacturer is Ifor Williams and you can find more information on their trailer range at www.iwt.co.uk.

The advantage of choosing this option is that buying a box trailer is relatively cheap. Also, a box trailer does not require taxing, servicing or an annual inspection such as an MOT. In

addition to this being a cheaper option for you to get started, a box trailer will help if you are pushed for storage space. However, storing all of your goods in a transportable device such as a trailer will possibly leave you with a security risk. If you choose this option, you should ensure that your trailer is always stored securely to avoid the risk of theft.

Sign writing on your van or trailer

Sign writing on your vehicle or trailer can be a great way of advertising your business cheaply. A colourful and eye-catching design with your company logo, address, web address, and contact details will be sure to get you noticed. It also reassures your customers that your business is professional and organised. This can cost as little as £75 and you should obtain several quotes before committing. A good place to start in finding a sign writer is www.yell.com or you can search the Internet.

If you do not wish to have permanent sign writing on your vehicle or trailer, you could opt for magnetic sign writing. This option is slightly cheaper than traditional sign writing and gives you the added advantage of removing the advertisement whenever you wish. Care should be taken when choosing magnetic vehicle signs as some suppliers' products lose their ability to stick to the vehicle after a lot of use.

THE FORM OF YOUR BUSINESS

Before you can really get going you need to give due consideration to the form of your business. Will you be a limited company or a sole trader? What about taxes and VAT? These are some of the questions you will need to ask yourself. The following paragraphs will help you to decide.

Sole Trader or Limited Company?

When setting up your business you will need to decide whether you want to be a sole trader or a limited company.

Sole Trader

A sole trader is essentially a self-employed individual and normally the proprietor of the business. Basically, a self-employed or sole trader is a named individual who will need to be identified on all business papers. For example, if your company is trading as 'John's Building & Maintenance', the proper entity when dealing with finances and government communications would be John Smith trading as John's Building & Maintenance.

Self-employed or sole traders are liable to self assessment tax and National Insurance payments, and you can find information and advice at www.hmrc.gov.uk.

Self assessment tax – This is paid on annual income less allowances (personal tax code) and expenses that are specific to running your business.

National Insurance – In being self-employed you do not lose the benefits of the National Health Service, providing you maintain your National Insurance payments relative

to your earnings. Most self-employed people pay Class 2 National Insurance, which is a very small amount of £2.20 per week. Class 4 National Insurance is also payable on annual profits between £5,225 and £34,840 at a rate of 8%. More information and advice can be found at www.hmrc.gov.uk.

Being self-employed offers advantages in the administration of your business as it can be less time-consuming and simpler than running a limited company. There are many, readily available, small business bookkeeping templates and books, which you can use to record your business income, costs and expenses. Alternatively, you could simply keep all your receipts, invoices, etc., and employ a small business accountant or bookkeeper to keep your books. Small business accountants normally charge between £10 and £15 per week, which will get you 3 meetings and your annual accounts and your tax return prepared, as well as advice on helping you to reduce your tax bill.

Liability – a sole trader is personally responsible for all amounts owed to any creditors and also any debts due to the Government. This means if you are unable to make suitable or sufficient arrangements to settle any of your debts, your personal possessions (including your residential property – your home) could possibly be taken to pay creditors. Where residential property is jointly owned, 50% could be claimed to pay creditors.

Limited company

Forming a limited company is not a long and complicated process and is actually relatively simple to achieve. A limited company is required to have a minimum of two company

directors, one of whom may act as Company Secretary, and shareholders. The primary reason for small business owners to become limited is the limited liability which is given to its directors. In addition to this, being a limited company is often perceived more positively and clients will often deal more comfortable with a company which is 'Limited'.

It would be wrong to think that credit (from both suppliers and banks) is more readily available to a limited company. Banks will not lend to any limited company where they cannot secure the debt against company assets such as premises, machinery, plant, stock, etc. However, banks will often lend to a limited company where the directors have some surety such as equity in their own home, bank account, insurance policies, etc. Lending and security of this nature will often lead to personal guarantees by the directors against their personal assets.

Often the banks will want a list of assets secured against that lending where business assets are used and/or where private assets are used. This is often undertaken for any lending or overdraft facility in excess of, say, £15,000. Suppliers will not normally require the same level of surety and will probably credit score your company and/or undertake a company search in order to ascertain your businesses credit worthiness.

The limited liability will only apply to the company directors. This is to help maintain the entrepreneurial spirit of small businesses who often contribute a huge amount to the British economy.

Once you are a limited company you have a legal responsibility to the Government and your employees. All registered companies must comply with legislation covering tax,

Income Tax, Corporation Tax, National Insurance, Health and Safety, Administration, and employment. Although directors may have the responsibility and liability for their actions and the company secretary is a very responsible position and one that authorities will look into it any trading accounts are not filed or late submissions to Companies House.

Tax and National Insurance

As the owner of a limited company you will pay yourself a salary, which will be subject to PAYE. You will have to complete a self-assessment tax form  each year, to determine whether any other taxes are due from the company, and any benefits you have received in your position as a director. The company must also deduct PAYE from any employees under your employment.

Company profits are taxed by system known as Corporation Tax. For example, if your company profit is between £1 and £300,000, this will be subject to 20% Corporation Tax. More information on Corporation Tax can be obtained from www.hmrc.gov.uk.

A limited company will also have a responsibility to deduct National Insurance from all employees including directors and also employees' National Insurance contributions. This will, in effect, increase your National Insurance contribution and is often overlooked when forming a limited company. More advice can be obtained from www.hmrc.gov.uk.

Depending on the number of employees you have, there may be a requirement for you to undertake arranging a stakeholder pension for employees. You should seek professional advice

on this issue as the fine for non-compliance is substantial. More advice can be obtained on this subject from www.thepensionservice.gov.uk.

Forming the company

You can form your limited company online at Companies' House – www.compaineshouse.gov.uk, where you will find the facility to choose a company name and see which names are already taken before you register your company. Alternatively, you can use a company formation agent, who will often offer other services such as bank accounts, business stationery, etc. You can search the web to find a company formation agent by entering 'form a limited company' in the search engine and a selection of agents will appear.

INSIDE TIP

*Be careful on your choice of company formation agent (if you choose this option) as there are many companies that charge well in excess of the Companies House fee. Setting up your limited company should cost no more than around £30. Often, these agents will offer lots of deals, so be sure you **read the small print** and if it sounds too good to be true, it probably is!*

We recommend you take professional advice when starting a limited company and ensure that you discuss the matter with a business consultant or with a fully qualified accountant.

VAT (Value added tax) registration

A sole trader or limited company can be VAT registered for Value Added Tax regardless of annual turnover, but *must* be registered for VAT if:

- at the end of any month the total value of the taxable supplies that you traded in the past 12 months or less more than £64,000, or

- at the time you expect that the value of your taxable supplies will be more than £64,000

(Please note that you should refer to www.hmrc.gov.uk for current information as this may change at any time)

Registering for VAT allows you to claim VAT on purchases, allowing you to recoup the VAT on all start-up equipment and supplies, which can be very helpful. Being VAT registered can also make a difference as to whether some suppliers or customers will deal with you. Being VAT registered also gives the impression to potential customers that you are a large company and, therefore, a professional organisation to deal with. You can obtain more information on becoming VAT registered at www.hmrc.gov.uk.

Again, when forming a company, we recommend that you seek professional advice from an accountant or business consultant. There can be many varying factors which could impact on whether you trade as a sole trader or as a limited company and an accountant or business specialist will be able to consider your personal and business circumstances before making any recommendations.

BANKING AND FINANCES

Obtaining Your Bank Account

There are many different options when obtaining your business bank account. Before deciding on which type of bank account you require, and its provider, you will, of course, need to have decided on the name of your business and also whether you will be a limited company, a sole trader, or a partnership.

Before you approach the bank, you will also need to decide what access you want. For example, will you require multiple signatories and cheque-books as well as cards or are you simply going to manage the bank accounts yourself?

You may need to consider the facilities which the bank account may offer. For example, will you wish to take credit card payments over the phone, in person, or over the Internet? You will also need to decide on whether you will require a cheque-book and cheque guarantee card and whether you will require a company credit card and Internet access to your business banking.

Many people prefer to pay by cheque or debit or credit card so it is often wise for your business to have the ability to accept these methods of payment.

Company credit cards

A company credit card is a great way for you to buy goods or services for your business over the Internet or in person over the counter and can often help your cash flow. However, it is wise to check the terms and conditions of these credit cards prior to entering into an agreement with your lender.

We recommend that you discuss this issue with your banker or financial advisor.

Internet banking

Most lenders offer Internet banking services for businesses, which is a good way to manage your business finances 24 hours a day / seven days a week and can often be a fast and convenient way managing your bank account and cash flow.

Telephone banking

In addition to the Internet banking services provided by most high-street banks, many also offer telephone banking, which can be very useful and convenient when you are running an active and busy business. This allows you to speak to your bank at any time of the day or night, as a lot of these services are a 24-hour operation and can, in addition, also act as a backup for your Internet banking should your connection prove difficult or problematic.

We recommend that you search the Internet to compare the business banking offers that are available. You will need to compare the high street banks and the accounts they offer to decide which would be the most suitable for your business. For example, in order to attract your business, one bank may offer free business banking, say, for up to 2 years to enable your business to get off the ground, while another bank might offer other incentives. We always recommend that you seek independent and professional advice and certainly shop around before you choose your bank.

GETTING YOUR MONEY IN

Make your terms of payment clear

In all of your agreements or contracts, you need to make your terms of payment very clear. For example, do you want payment within, say, 14 days or 30 days; will you charge interest after a certain period of time, etc? Your terms of payment must also be made clear to your customers or clients in order to ensure that you receive your money.

Use every opportunity you can to make the terms of payment both clear and concise. If you are selling services online, you can ask your customer to check or tick a box online to accept the terms and conditions of payment. You will be very surprised at how many businesses do not do this.

Invoices

If you are required to invoice your customer or client for the services or products you have delivered, your invoice should clearly show how much is due, when it is due and how the charge is made up. Getting the information wrong can delay payment of the invoice, as, in some circumstances, the customer may require a revised invoice.

It is important to get this right as your customer may need accurate invoices for day-to-day expenses of their company. Invoices can be sent by post, faxed or even emailed (electronic invoicing).

It is also good to send out reminders promptly for unpaid invoices, but you will need to ensure that you do not strain your relationship with your customer. If you stick to your terms of business, everyone knows where they are!

Electronic Invoicing

Electronic invoicing can be very effective and save both time and money. No stamps, no postage and no paper, less printer cartridges/printing costs. This is the most cost effective way of invoicing.

In addition to this, there are many other added benefits to this form of invoicing, as follows:

- Secure electronic delivery

- Confirmed electronic delivery

- Reduce days sales outstanding

- Reduced print and postage costs

- Reduced requirement for sending out copy invoices

- Faster dispute resolution

- Faster turnaround

- Improved filing

- Easier to duplicate details on similar invoices

- Workflow patterns in software for checking of data

- Easier to amend or alter invoices

When using electronic invoicing, you must ensure that your customer is able to receive this form of invoicing. Be sure to ask the question before assuming that your customer can accept electronic invoicing.

It is also important to protect the authenticity of the invoice when sending it electronically. Your invoices should either be written into an email itself, attached as a protected word file or sent as a pdf document.

Keep the invoice and communication layout the same and use delivery tracking to check that your email has arrived safely. It is also wise to ask your customers or clients to let you know of any communication they might receive and which they suspect may be fraudulent.

As with any electronic data, you should ensure that your information is backed up regularly and is secure. We advise that you seek advice from a technical expert on these issues to ensure that your information is safe and secure.

Cash

This is the oldest and most well-known form of payment and goes back centuries; even taxes used to be collected in this way. However, keeping large amounts of cash can often be dangerous and pose a security risk to your company. In addition to this, there is also the issue of collecting cash. For some businesses, accepting cash is the only way to complete the sale. For example, if you are running a sweet shop, you would probably prefer cash payment.

It is inevitable that some of your customers will wish to pay in cash and you should not discourage this method of payment. Cash has the advantage of being an immediate payment method and ensures that your money is guaranteed as soon as it is handed to you.

We recommend that any cash that you receive should be fully documented and banked as quickly as possible in order to reduce any risk to the business and individuals handling the cash. When accepting payments in cash, you should always ensure that any currency is checked for counterfeit notes. It is also wise to record the denominations that make up the

cash payment to ensure that your staff are aware of how you record payment in this method. You must also ensure that receipt of payment is recorded in your accounting practices in order that it can be included within the day-to-day running of the business.

Cheques and paying in

Cheques are one of the most tried and tested methods of payment and have been around for a long time. Cheques are still in use today and are still a popular method of payment for many individuals and companies. There is no doubt that over the coming years the chequebook will become redundant and your business should prepare for this by using alternative payment methods such as debit/credit card transactions.

Accepting payment by cheque can be a disadvantage to your company because cheques need to be paid into the bank and then take several days to go through the clearing system. In addition to this, it is quite common for individuals or companies to make a mistake in writing out a cheque, which then needs to be rectified before you can receive payment.

The clearing system works within a three working day period, so it will take several days longer to receive payment over holiday periods or weekends.

First day – Your cheque is paid into the business account (at your bank). It is then sent to the bank's clearing centre at the end of the working day.

Second day – The cheque is then sorted at the bank's clearing centre and the details are taken from the cheque including the amount. These are then sent electronically to the bank on which they are to be drawn (the payee's bank). The physical cheque is then sent on to the bank which will be paying the amount (the payee's bank).

Third day – The payee's bank takes the amount from your customer's bank account. At the same time, all banks calculate the amount they must pay each other based on the activity of the previous day. All balances are then reconciled across all banks.

I think it is clear to see why this system is being phased out, due to its lengthy process!

Inside tips on receiving payment

Here are some general tips on how to improve your chances of getting paid and getting paid promptly. The following is not an exhaustive list and advice should always be sought from financial experts, but some clear guidance is always welcome:

- Look around for a business account that provides the best level of service for your business needs. Different banks have different policies on receiving or making payments.

- Ensure you know the creditworthiness of your customers or clients in order to minimise the risk of not getting paid. For high value payments, this is essential. Consider getting credit checks on customers or clients that use you regularly or are likely to run up large accounts. You can get credit checks from variety of

credit reference agencies on the Internet on sites such as www.equifax.co.uk or www.experian.co.uk which are the two leading providers in the UK. The cost is very small in comparison to the risk associated with taking on bad credit risks.

- Undertake a company search on any large organisations that you are doing business with. One of the most reliable and trustworthy sources is www.companieshouse.gov.uk. Some information on the site is free if you decide not to take out a full search. It is good, for instance, to know how long a company has been in business for.

- Consider using more secure methods of payment such as CHAPS (guaranteed same-day payment of cleared funds in the UK) or credit card/debit card payments or even systems such as PayPal, etc.

- Pay all forms of payment into your account as soon as possible to ensure that you have the money banked and not laying around.

- Consult your bank on the best payment method when dealing with foreign customers, as foreign cheques cannot always be cleared through the UK cheque systems and they can also attract high fees to process too. You also need to be aware of exchange rates and keep any eye out for fluctuations in currency values.

Gift Cards/vouchers or loyalty schemes

These are a great way for your customers to forward purchase your goods or services. If your business is able to provide gift vouchers or gift certificates, we recommend that you organise your business so that these can be utilised by your customers.

All you need to do is simply devise a process for accepting and processing these gift vouchers or certificates, and, of course, be sure they cannot be fraudulently replicated or reused. You can find many different designs related to gift cards at www.vistprint.co.uk, which can be in traditional card form, credit card style or even electronic.

These could also be linked to reward or loyalty schemes, which offer free gifts or services in order to entice customers to use, and continue using, your services. This has proved very successful for major retailers such as Tesco, Sainsbury's and many other high street names.

INSIDE TIP

First, you need to ensure that your business can utilise and accept these forms of payment. You should clearly outline the terms and conditions associated with any loyalty scheme or gift vouchers. They will need to be presented in a particular format and you will almost certainly require a notice period and also an expiry date is often wise. When undertaking schemes such as this, is always good to seek professional advice and also, if necessary, a legal view on the terms and conditions attached to any loyalty or gift voucher scheme.

Electronic Bank Payment

Another popular, ever increasing, method of payment is electronic banking, which is now widely used by individuals and businesses – the Internet has revolutionised the way in which banking can be done, online. Electronic payments are produced, either by you or a third party acting on your behalf, and transmitted to the banking system, which undertakes the transfer of funds for you.

This method of transferring money is referred to as 'Direct Credit', and can be used for paying for almost anything these days. There are many advantages to this method of payment:

- Reduces late payment of invoices
- Reduces payment periods
- Saves postage, travelling and queuing time and costs
- Regular payments can be fully automated
- Regular reporting of payments received
- Improved cash flow
- Simpler and more effective accounting
- Immediate clearance
- Can even be checked on mobiles
- Text alerts to your mobile phone when paid
- Professional image

In order for this method to work, you will need to provide the details of your bank account so that a payment can be made

from your customer's/client's bank to your own. Clearly, your customers or clients will also need to have an evening facility with their bank or building society in order for this to work.

You are advised to follow your own bank's processes in order to ensure that the details you provide are secure and in line with your bank's policy when receiving these payments. You are advised to contact your bank or building society for any advice related to this method of payment.

Customer Accounts

Where you have regular customers who buy your goods or services frequently, you could opt to provide your customers with an account. Essentially you are offering them credit on the goods or services which you are supplying. Clearly, you need to research your customers and clients to establish a credit history to minimise any risk to your business.

In order for this to work effectively, you will need to set up a very organised and comprehensive accounting system. You are advised to seek professional advice as there are many different methods and systems you can use. In addition to this, there are also many software providers that offer platforms for you to operate customer accounts. They should be experienced and knowledgeable in the operating and running of such accounts in order for them to be effective for your business.

Invoice Factoring

Invoice factoring works for businesses where there are customers or clients who take up to 60 days to pay their invoices. However, you don't want to lose them by turning

away business because their payment terms do not suit you. Having slow paying clients is commonplace in today's environment. This makes managing cash flow very difficult, especially where your supplier's terms are not the same as your clients! Factoring of your invoices is a way of solving this problem by getting paid faster as it is a financing tool that allows you to get your invoices paid quickly. It provides your business with the necessary working capital to operate the business and can help your cash flow.

Factoring involves selling your invoices at a discount in order to receive payment sooner. The factoring company waits to get paid by your clients, while you get almost immediate payment of your invoices.

Essentially, you deliver goods or services and invoice for them as normal. Your business then sells the invoice to the factoring company, following which they will pay your business 70% to 90% of the invoice value. This advance is paid very quickly, which obviously helps with your cash flow. The 'factor' then chases payment from your customer and, once they have paid, they pay your business the balance (10% to 30%, dependent upon their initial payment to you). Your business is then charged a fee, often referred to as a 'rebate', for the transaction. Factoring costs can vary, but are generally up to 3% of the invoice value per month.

The advantages of factoring invoices are outlined below:

- Fast payment
- Better business cash flow
- Better opportunity for borrowing
- Improved credit rating

- Improved expansion possibilities

- Improved relationship with clients

- Better purchasing power

- Improved borrowing opportunities

Most factoring can be set up in about a week. The biggest requirement for approval is that do you do business with credit-worthy clients, thus reducing the risk to the factoring company.

We recommend that you scan the market for competitive terms and seek professional advice from a financial expert before signing up to any agreements.

Credit & debit cards

Taking card transactions over the Internet

 Most High Street banks will enable you to take debit and credit card transactions over the telephone, in person or over the Internet with one of their card schemes. However, there are many card transaction companies that you could add to your website to enable you to take payments over the Internet. Many of these providers will charge for this and generally charge per transaction and not a flat monthly fee. These can be very beneficial to your business enabling you to set them up very easily and quickly to enable your Internet site to work hard for you by taking payments. A common provider is www.paypal.co.uk where no upfront charges or monthly fees are charged for the basic merchant service.

────────

INSIDE TIP

Always take advice from a professional or financial expert when considering matters of a financial nature. You can talk to your bank or financial advisor or, alternatively, you can seek advice from the Financial Services Authority or the Institute of Financial Advisers in order to ensure that you are seeking advice from the right individuals.

Free letters and forms

Should you need to seek advice on getting paid, or if you would simply like to make yourself aware of the legislation and processes around pursuing late payment of invoices, there are lots of organisations and advice online.

Clearly, the best way to resolve any dispute is to come to an understanding with your customer and client with regard to getting paid without taking any formal action. However, there are times when the only option is to pursue formal action and you should seek advice from your Citizen's Advice Bureau, specialist company lawyers or solicitors, who can advise you on pursuing bad debts or unpaid invoices.

It is advisable to set up your business so that you are organised in advance should you need to pursue any debts to your business. A good site for information is www.payontime.co.uk, where you will find explanations and standard forms in addition to advice on legislation and practices relating to pursuing payment. Other sources of information could be your local Chamber of Commerce www.britishchambers.org.uk or Federation of Small Businesses www.fsb.org.uk.

Business launch or open day

When you have your business set up and you are organised, it is always a good idea to have an open day or launch event not only to celebrate the fact that you have started your business but also to provide a great opportunity for you to market a launch in the local community.

Think about the type of people you would like to invite and also events that will help you to market and promote your business. For example, if you are opening a catering business, why not tap into a community event where you can provide free samples of your food and products to potential customers and clients.

INSIDE TIP

Remember, these events can be classed as marketing and advertising expenses, the cost of which can be offset against any business profit you may make later in the year.

Ensure that you make the most of the launch event and distribute as many leaflets and freebies as your business can afford, letting people know where they can contact you and purchase your goods or services from. The event does not have to be expensive and can be very beneficial in establishing your business and attracting potential business.

INSIDE TIP

In order to attract a crowd, it is said that you need crowds to attract one. So, invite your friends and family to the launch, which will help to create a buzz

*and interest in your products and services, as people
will naturally assume that the level of interest has
been created around your product or service and its
reputation.*

Grants and funding

In some circumstances your business may be able to benefit
from community grants, local authority grants, sponsorship
and environmental grants or subsidised loans and lending.
This will depend upon your business sector and the area in
which you wish to operate your business. For example, you
might be eligible for a 0% interest loan from The Carbon
Trust for equipment that could reduce carbon footprint of
your business. Particular criteria will often have to be met but
don't discount these grants as some can be of benefit to your
business.

You may also be able to sponsor your business by promoting
another business's supplies or services. For example, if you
are a mobile hairdressing or beauty business, you might be
able to establish a link with a supplier to share marketing
opportunities.

Getting free advice

There are many organisations that will be happy to provide you
with free advice relating to your business sector and setting
up your business. For example, banks or building societies
will often give free advice, DVDs and leaflets to assist you in
setting up and running your business effectively. Make the
most of these opportunities and gain all the knowledge you
can from these sources.

Industry bodies, such as professional institutes or associations, within your business sector can provide you with free pamphlets and advice which can help you to set up and run your business. Contact your local association, institute or manufacturing organisation for information and also ask for any opportunities for free training which could benefit your business.

Suppliers will also often offer free advice on training and use of new products, especially if they are trying to promote and launch a particular system or product in your selected industry. These events can also provide the opportunity to network with like-minded people and you may meet new contacts or business associates and, you never know, you may even learn something!

Search the Internet for free courses, information and offers relating to your business sector to source products or services that will help make your business a success.

Keep track of your costs

When starting your new business, it is very easy to become very enthusiastic and excited about your new venture. This can often lead to you purchasing materials and products and services which you may not really require. Remember, your business needs to be profitable and you should keep control of your expenditure and spend wisely. Ensure that you have a complete list of what you need with regard to stock, stationery, materials, etc., in order for your business to get up and running. You can always invest in the bells and whistles and more expensive items of equipment when your business is more established.

INSIDE TIP

*Remember to **keep all your receipts** and keep track of your expenditure as not only is it information you will need to pass on to your accountant or bookkeeper, but it will also help you to 'keep your eye on the ball' financially. It is easy to forget to keep that receipt for the book of stamps that you bought or for the fuel that you bought to fill up your vehicle. Ensure that you remain focused about keeping and recording all of your expenditure.*

CONCLUSION

We hope that you have enjoyed reading this guide and that you found the information contained within the guide useful and informative. We are constantly updating our guides and release new issues frequently. If you have any good ideas or observations, please let us know.

We wish you every success in your new business venture and hope that you have a profitable and enjoyable time starting and running your own **Cleaning Business**.

how2become

Visit www.how2become.com
for more business titles and
career guides